Rapunzel's Hair

Poems by Judi Rypma

All Nations Press
Copyright 2006 Judi Rypma

Rapunzel's Hair

First Edition

Library Card Catalogue Data On Reserve
ISBN 0-977954-0-3

All Nations Press
PO Box 601
White Marsh, VA 23183
www.allnationspress.com

Contents

Hungry Women 5
Gretel's 8
That Cottage 12
Rapunzel's Hair 14
Sleeping Beauty 16
Goldilocks 18
The Little Mermaid Loses 21
That Queen 24
Baba Yaga 29
The Handless Maiden 33
Gluttony 35
Red Shoes 38

ACKNOWLEDGMENTS:

Grateful acknowledgment is made to the publications in which the following poems first appeared:

"Baba Yaga"　　*Birmingham Poetry Review*
"Gluttony"　　*Coe Review*
"Goldilocks"　　*The Amherst Review*
"The Little Mermaid Loses"　*The Amherst Review*

HUNGRY WOMEN

"Their hunger became so great that their mother became unhinged and desperate.
Indeed, she said to her children, 'I've got to kill you so I can have something to eat!'"

>"The Children of Famine"
><u>Household Tales</u>
>by the Brothers Grimm, 1815 ed.

When the famines came
wispy peasants lined country roads--
corpses
ignored as if they were scarecrows
overseeing fields. Straw
stuffed between their teeth
       testimony to a Last Supper

so who could blame all those women
       a ravenous coven
concerned with culinary matters:

Rapunzel's mother trading a daughter
for a taste of lettuce.

Baba Yaga bingeing
on sautéed kids   skull-on-a-stick
kidney and eggs on rye.

Sleeping Beauty's mother-in-law
longing to gorge herself on
her grandchildren
fooled by a chef
        boiled to death by her son.

Gretel pilfering candy windows
until the lady of the house rebelled
grabbed Hansel for revenge
        stocked up on Open Pit.

They never knew if it was Persephone's
pomegranate craving
        or Eve and that stupid apple

who started the shopping list
doomed us to six months of cold
nine months of ripening bodies

set a precedent
       for famished women
believing they must
taste and nibble

    gobble and devour

          eat or be eaten
feed an insatiable craving--
emptiness that may never be filled.

GRETEL'S WITCH

I.

Why were they out there   nibbling
what took so long to create? Months
carving candy balustrades and eaves.
Years pummeling dough,
hauling confectioner's paste   and *ah*
those peppermint panes, licorice
fence posts, pancake-paved paths.

The chimney alone took me weeks--
peanut brittle squares placed just so,
a gingerbread scarecrow
perched on Necco wafer shingles
to frighten crows and squirrels. Countless
afternoons buttering, baking drywall
         sweet security.

I didn't mind scrimping in retirement
and when those brats showed up
feigned politeness, invited them to share.

But that girl--so greedy, sure
the world owed her what parents
wouldn't deliver   no wonder
they ditched her

and the boy--cocky, following her
without protest when she suggested stealing:
first frosted chunks of my house
then jewels stashed for medical bills

      so I stuffed him in a cage
so he couldn't eat me
out of house and home.

II.
Thought the little chap would be safe there
till I fattened him up to send home
but his bony fingers stayed thin as twigs
so I emptied the pantry   cut into pastry portals.
Still the girl wouldn't pull her weight
      grew porker plump
nosed around for something to swipe
and I vowed to get them out of there
before losing a life's savings.

The day she convinced me to bake cookies
as if she hadn't sucked the sugar supply,
chewed holes in the walls
left us all shivering. I ordered her
inside the stove   to keep warm
but she pretended it wasn't working
     and I climbed in to investigate.

III.

They are gone   fleeing on my pet duck
     (*a l'Orànge* by now)
while the imps flourish beyond the forest
squandering my family heirlooms
telling lies between chocolate bars
selling my house plans to *Architectural Digest*
passing on a sugar-coated version of what they
did to those prim Grimms
who habitually transformed old women
into crones and hags   to please
the royal one they dared not insult

and I, reduced to ashes,
memory of me burnt to cinders
     cry out only in stories

though no one hears
      between the lines.

THAT COTTAGE

Late at night poring through
Better Homes and Gardens
she always finds it--
marshmallow crème facade
gingerbread trim
wrought licorice fencing

same one she's searched for her entire life
don't we all
yearn for candied cottages
ice cream fantasies
       chocolate chip lives

but now
hunched over a candy cane
moving slowly   sonorously
through Rest Haven's sterile, overheated
corridors
her blurred eyes seek out
Mother's Day bingo
where she might win a Hershey bar

and determined   she reaches out to feel
one thin finger
knowing its plumpness
could stave off the end
prevent
      baked old hag.

RAPUNZEL'S HAIR

It grew
and grew--
flaxen waves
undulating
across grain fields visible from
the tower to which she was
condemned because of a mother's
appetite for lettuce. Years later the prince

climbed
those locks
as if they were beanstalks
satiated his hunger, reaped
the harvest of silken tassels
ravished that golden body

until the witch ended
the growing season
chopping the tresses
the way you slice and dice
salad fixings

and instead of
a corn maiden
the girl ripened
into a helpless
yellow squash--
extended belly
swollen breasts
short-stemmed head.

Desperate
she shoved the old woman
out the window
splattered her
like a pumpkin

which earned Rapunzel
another crown
to replace
that glorious one she lost

and a chance to trade
the tower for
a prince's castle--
one prison
for another.

SLEEPING BEAUTY

What if the man who kissed her
had been the wrong one

like the woman in the chapel
presented with a gold ring
on a satin pillow
awaiting those five words:
you may kiss the bride
so she lets him lift the lace veil
presses warm lips to his

never suspecting that
when she awakens
(maybe years from now)
she will discover

a rose-petaled life
has grown into a thorn hedge.
That he is
no prince. That
another curse
has been placed on her.

That she wishes
she could snuggle
under the blankets
alone. Sleep
for another hundred years.

GOLDILOCKS

That's what they called me
back when
    I was welcome in strange beds
invited to tables   to partake
of something more delicious than porridge

refused to don glasses
didn't realize men were wolves
in bears' clothing.

I didn't need a key
to the apartment, condo, mobile home
    was greeted lustily at three or seven or eleven

and no one said
"don't touch my bowl"
but stuffed me with grapes, oysters
stroked toasted golden skin
tasted tawny limbs
    not too sweet, not too salty

and no one hollered
"Who's been sleeping in my bed?"
but slid me beneath the sheets
where I craved
getting eaten up.

That was when Mama and Papa Bear
didn't mind letting baby cuddle
with me   though later
they growled "Harlot"
threatened to cut him from the will
until I fled out the window
knowing my Bear would eventually forget
    the taste of honey.

    Still I kept knocking on doors
in search of an empty house
to call home
or a baby bear
(black, brown, grizzly, polar,
an occasional panda)
as long as he was free
might invite me in
to pronounce him "just right."

But that was then.

                "Graylocks," they'd say now

accuse me of gumming their bowls
leaking on the chair:
"Call the police, Papa Bear.
Some crone's been sleeping in our beds
    and by God the thing is still there."

THE LITTLE MERMAID LOSES

Inspired by a single wet kiss
she spurned sapphire sand
amber windows   enchanted kingdom
of pink weeping willows
coral castles
crimson flowers
    for another kind of red.

Silly girl. Dodging eels. Risking life
to swim to a swamp witch
who sucked snakes. Lined sailors' bones
    in an underwater trophy case--
an overbosomed underwater Baba Yaga
giving customers what they wanted
in a pawn shop of lust.

Not that the *mer* girl needed encouragement,
resolved to unfasten the chastity belt of fins
agree to anything for a honeymoon
with a stranger--one short lifetime
    when she could have spent three
hundred years
in aquatic paradise.

So the deed was done: one tongue
snipped with a flick of the blade--
no more karaoke nights
gabfests with the sisters
solos on the rocks   and in return
        a chance
at the oxymoron: love and marriage.

The hag wasn't obligated to offer
a warranty   but did promise
perpetually bleeding feet
leg pain fierce as the slash of sword blades
no more dancing with oysters
cavorting with turtles
Hide and Seek behind coral heads.

No matter, the mermaid thought
dreaming of the night
her new hymen
        would split open like a lobster shell

and the earth prince
would pierce flesh
without knowing   or caring

the crustacean
had sacrificed a life
so he could get that first taste
of sweet meat   savor
            buttery wet seafood.

That Queen

I.

The story's not as clear
as that Looking Glass
reassuring her she was Fair
    most Just in the land

especially with a stepdaughter from hell
disguised   by gobs of white powder
pouty lips slathered with Revlon Blood Red
when she finally seduced the huntsman
with a Lolita crush
    lured him into the forest
a nubile tease pressing Snow White skin
to his weathered body
    before threatening to cry rape to the queen.

He panicked, paid what she asked
    especially when she hinted at a baby
fabricated a story
to explain her absence.

Of course the queen grieved
      presented with a pile of organs
the word of a loyal employee who claimed
he misinterpreted her wishes,
cited Henry II's erroneous Becket execution
as precedent.

She tried to get on with her life
covered ears with jeweled hands
when the mirror informed her
the girl was alive--
      shacked up with seven men.

II.

This was a woman who
took mothering duties seriously
had to know the truth
so she resorted to
      masks, distortions, subterfuge
what any parent of a wayward teen must

offered the ungrateful wretch   a comb
to untangle dyed ebony hair,
    lace   to cover an immodest bodice,

>   half of a Delicious apple
> to guard her health
>
> but soon as the relieved queen departed
>   the little bitch choked on her greed.
>
> Back home the woman tended the castle
> tried not to worry
> didn't dare tell her husband the truth:
> his daughter lived,
>   liked to do things in groups.
>
> Meanwhile the little men   relieved
> (night after night they had argued,
>   took turns
> cleaning   to justify her existence)
> didn't have the strength left
> to dig a hole. Instead they slid her
> between two window panes
> where they could gaze at her every day,
> ask themselves, "Who's the dumbest
>   of them all?"
> remember what they'd lost
>   and gained.
> She posed for them--no longer

venomous, still gorgeous,
rendered harmless in sleep--
      a dead insect pinned in a glass display

III.

Months passed   and some dude showed up
    obviously into necrophilia
since he bid on the corpse
paid the dwarfs to tote the glass sandwich
to his swanky mountain home.

Seven short out-of-shape guys
terrified someone might accuse them
of defiling their willing royal guest
slipped in the mud
forcing   the apple chunk to burst
from her hearty lungs--a dangerous projectile

and she started chattering
    in medieval Valley Girl.

The dwarfs cringed, ran
back to the mines, prayed the prince

wouldn't return her
>   but men don't hear what they don't want to.
To this guy her shrillness sounded sweet
and he shut her up
>   with his lips, tongue
begged her to marry him
without a prenuptial contract, before
he thought it out
insisted on inviting her family.

Snow White agreed, of course,
even promised to furnish her stepmom's wardrobe
>   complete with a special pair of shoes
and we know the rest:

how the poor old woman danced until   flames
licked her arches, then ankles
and she perished--
>   a martyr burned at the foot
for crimes she never committed.

BABA YAGA

Building that fence of bones
   (femurs make the best posts,
   jaws the strongest latches,
   metatarsals the smoothest hinges)
I knew there would be trouble--

so much effort to keep nosy urchins out
      as if I didn't deserve a little privacy
after centuries of labor

but *they* swiped the skulls
   as if they were playthings
batted them around
with my broom, chanted taunts from afar
teased the cats   and me.

    It took that fib
I let slip over vodkas
with Koshchei--that I preferred
blood cocktails
      had a hankering for maiden *mignon*.

That evil lout never could keep his trap shut
    so now they all dodge my place
no matter which forested spot I choose--

less stress on my chicken's legs
weary from trying to hold up the hut
    heavier each year
as I add new recipes:
    Heavenly Hair and Hands Hash,
    Seven Ways to Sweeten Bone Stew
    Appendix-on-Rye Sandwiches,
    Ten Steps to Tastier Toes
arrange them around my roasting pot
when lost travelers stop by.

Lies always blow through the land
    faster than any wind I could conjure
so now I can relax, weave for hours
without hearing children screech.

Just as well, since these days
I tire, get dizzy, prefer not
to sail around in the mortar

instead wanted those chicken legs so badly
to move the hut to and fro--

never anticipated

the nausea   nor
how itching gums could drive me
to gnaw on birch trunks,
sharpen molars on the thickest branches--
endless toothaches
no apothecary can ease
          for iron fangs and bicuspids
.
Rheumatism makes housekeeping impossible
     so I raid villages for maidens
(no one cleans like a virgin)
who keep the place free of grime,
steal grain, pilfer thread and wood,
would shove me in the oven
if I didn't gnash my teeth
          or put the fear of the stew pot
into them.   Someday

one of them will win
will destroy me before
I pretend to fall for another phony story
    of blessings and magical gifts,
before I send her off with a doll, advice,
confidence

and then I will vanish   melting
    into the river of fire.

THE HANDLESS MAIDEN

Hush.
Can you hear her?   weeping
on the stumps of her arms--

a woman bathed in gold-white light,
boughs wilted, dismembered
not branching out
    no longer rooted.

The Devil--predator
of the psyche   gone
but not without taking
the maiden's somnolent soul

    so she'll wander the underground forest
in search of a flowering fruit tree--
        muddied moonlit woman
floating into the forbidden orchard,
    scurrying across the poisoned moat

and when she finds what she seeks
one twig will bend to her numb lips
so she can pluck the pear

                suck its sweetness
            ingest its seeds
            feed off the king's fruit trees
            until she is rescued
            or captured.   She will accept his royal offer
                of substitute sterling silver hands

            later do seven years of penance,
            await a second rescue

            until the day her wrists ache
            then itch
            as the stubs throw out tiny shoots--
                    finger blossoms
            that sprout   spread
            fast as weeds after a storm

            until the hands grow back
                into fuller, more resilient branches.
            She will use them for cradling babies,
            enfolding a husband to her bosom
                    fertilizing and nourishing
            but in all the stories you hear
            forgetting to ripen her reborn soul.

GLUTTONY

So many gastronomic adventures--
miniature consumers starved
for Happy Meals. Food missiles hurled
across cafeterias. Weekends ogling Hannibal
Lecter   risking victimless cannibalism

like Gretel feasting on a slab
of gingerbread drywall, double-pane
candy windows. Sweet tooth

inspiring an old woman slaving over a sugar
house
to take revenge in flesh
salivate over a plumpening finger,
         salting, stewing, envisioning
a juicier Hansel--basted boy at a barbecue
precipitated by one greedy girl

or Snow White sampling leftover round steak
swiped off the dwarves' plates
exonerated by days in the forest
trying to forget the queen had a craving
         for pickled lung and liver

but how to excuse the girl later--
belly full of groceries, seven benefactors
yet reaching for that juicy apple
        a fleshy breast   dangled
by someone eaten up with envy.

And Goldilocks guzzling that porridge--
first degree food theft
though the beneficent bears forgave her
for treating their home like a free Holiday Inn.

Jack, too, trading a perfectly good milk cow
for a handful of beans that promised
to sprout to epic proportions--become
        Jolly Green Giant of the vegetable world
yet he had to break in, raid
the ogre's kitchen, linger
over breakfast, let the wife
take the ultimate risk. Forced
to hide in the oven   almost
        Child on Toast
yet he returned again and again
for cash, goose, harp

when he could've been content--
sold more beans than Bird's Eye.

Only the Gingerbread Boy failed
to win riches, a princess, a castle
    all sacrificed when he fled
from one of the few sets of fairyland parents
who valued what they created,
    He made his own agony
racing through a world where everyone
yearned to taste him
        and was suitably devoured.

RED SHOES

> *"She confessed her sins and the executioner cut off her feet, and the red shoes danced away with them into the dark forest."*
> from Hans Christian Andersen's
> "The Red Shoes" translated by
> Erik Christian Haugaard

I.

Frantically twirling and tapping
she danced madly
     unable to cease her frantic jig
not knowing the devil had taken her feet, almost
won her soul

what you get for yearning to escape a life,
forgetting the price a woman pays
for coveting that bright red glow--

    sinful shade of ripened apples

passion   anger   vanity

like Snow White's stepmother
prancing to a ballroom death
in red-hot slippers, smoke curling
around her ankles			flames of hell
licking her toes, sparing her

the blood oozing from those stepsisters'
heels and toes, their desperate attempt
to squeeze into the glass slippers.
Who knows if Cinderella slipped so easily
	into the rest of her love-fired life
or if the prince beat her with a switch,
turned her flesh crimson, banished her
to a lifetime of ruddy hands, aching feet
	and an ash-strewn stove.